You never know where a new friend might pop up.

Spring *tiptoes* in,
stirring up earthy
smells, coaxing
color from the
winter-brown woods.

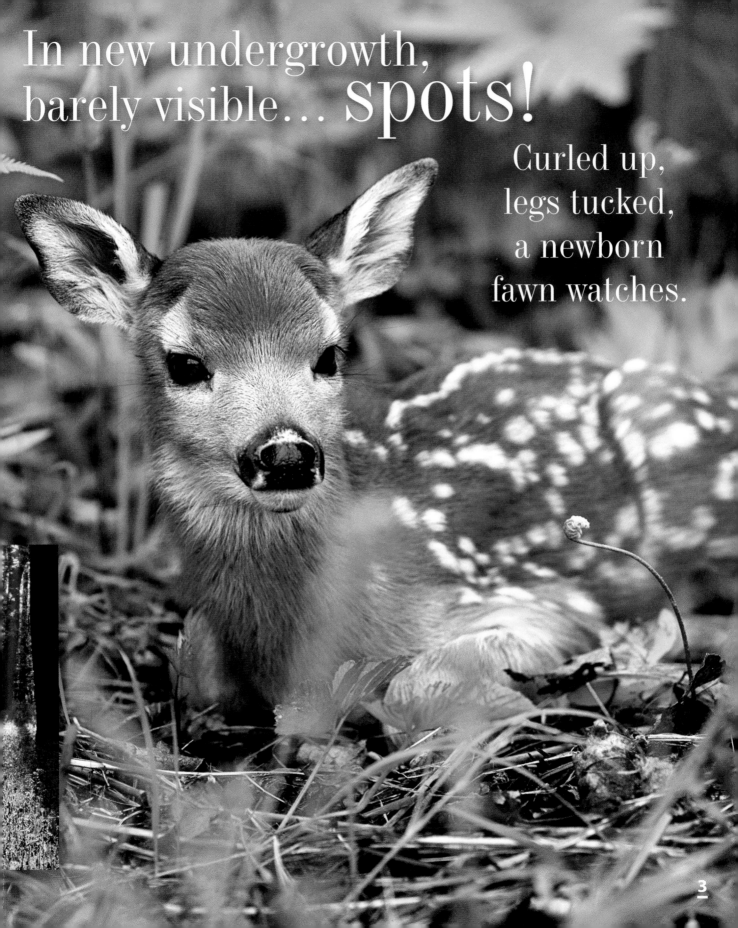

In new undergrowth, barely visible… spots!

Curled up, legs tucked, a newborn fawn watches.

Spring
nudges awake
slumbering
trees.

Leaves unfurl to hide fluffy nestlings
gobbling a buggy breakfast.

Spring pulls flowers
and rubbery mushrooms
from unexpected places.

Abracadabra!

Spring welcomes new arrivals.

Deep in the meadow grass,
velvety bunnies huddle,
noses twitch-twitch-twitching.

Fuzzy ducklings totter to a rippled pond.

Splish-splash!

In they go, webby
feet piddle-paddling.

Spring brings babies to the barnyard.
PEEP! PEEP! PEEP!
Hoppy yellow chicks explore beyond the nest.

Silken piglets root for breakfast.
SQUEET!

Spring scatters dandelions across a dewy hillside.

Wobbly lambs kick up their heels with new friends.

9

Spring turns trickles
to streams.

In a sheltered bend,
wiggly black tadpoles
wait, feeling froggier
by the day.

Spring urges seedlings in tidy gardens and rolling farmland to reach for the warmth awaiting them above ground…

...and invites wind-scattered seeds
to take root in her soft, damp soil.

Spring drags
a grey blanket
across the sky.

Plip – plop – plip.

Every creature
hurry-scurries
home to sit
tight…

till the rumbly
storm passes…

...and the spring-bright
sun shines again.